THROUGH THE EYES OF JOY BIRD

Poetry by,

J.K.W.

FORWARD

Dear Readers: This poetry journal conveys the heights and depths of my soul, as I have experienced life's many ups and downs. It is the work of my lifetime and creating this masterpiece and being willing to share it with all of you, was no easy task. Thank you for supporting me on my continued journey, by allowing me to share, even just a little bit of who I am, with you.   Not every poem is a life lesson I have gone through. Some are just fun poems from my imagination or poems about my hobbies or expressing my deep love of nature. Other poems are dark and deal with real issues like suicidal thoughts or the wracking pain of romantic, as well as familiar loss. Not every poem is based on real events or circumstances, but all my writings have been my outlet for what I have experienced in various stages of my life, starting in high school and ending with where I am at now, married and working. I hope you enjoy reading these as much as I have in writing them.

DEDICATION

To my loving husband of fourteen years and my family for supporting me in this endeavor.
You are the reason that I write. I also wish to thank every friend, ex, co-worker, and extended family
member whom I've made memories with. Besides my love of nature, and my various hobbies, it is you who
are the origination of my poetry, as I journaled away over the years, in prose.
Lastly, though first in my heart, thank you Lord for getting me through my darker days and helping me
change my sinful ways, as some of my sketchy/scary/ sinful endeavor etc. poetry will show, I've been
through a lot.

CONTENTS

POEMS OF NATURE

<u>What does a Horse Know? (1998)</u>

Who knows what the horse knows?

Could the birds know?

    They tell each other everything

    As they sing.

How could any other creature know what the horse knows?

No other creature is as majestic or as swift and wise

    As a horse is.

If you ever find out

What a horse has to say

Please tell me in the land of poetry.

    My address is:

The forest of dreams

Where kangaroos laugh

And hippos can sing.

But only the favored

Can hear their song.

Which of course,

Is the horse,

Appreciated by only the few.

To Rest

A mockingbird, dive-bombing a cat.

What's up with that?

Grabbing tufts of fur, for a nest.

Sneak attack.

The cat rolled on its back

And with talons extended, attacks

Now the bird may be laid to rest.

No longer able to feather its nest.

Unpardonable Sin

The crows must go

There's nothing left to hoe.

What's this; a bluebird?

Someone's going to pay

And rue the day

They took this life away.

The other birds

Can be heard

And **oh,** the screaming!

Unpardonable sin!

<u>"Red Feathered Breast"</u> (2003)

A robin fell from

    The sky

Smack, hit the pavement

    Feathers floating by

The warmth faded fast

    Soft, red-feathered breast

So fragile; so soft

    You once flew

Now your neck is broken

    You're going into shock.

And with one last convulsion

    You're small, beady eyes are locked

What made you fall,

    Little, red-feathered breast?

A loss of life, so delicate

    I'm helpless to assist.

Helpless ------

    I leave.

<u>Shadows</u> (2003)

Shadows in the pines

Dancing like leaves in my mind

Whither do they go?

I watch you as you sleep

Sometimes hidden from view

Yet all may look upon me

Because I never move

Who am I?

the moon

Up in a tree

Nocturnal, I be

My head it freely swivels

With large round eyes

I'm considered most wise

Who might I be?

an owl

<u>"Foxes"</u>

(2005)

Foxes dancing beneath the sky

Frolicking on graves of lives gone by

Must death always be

Looked upon so gravely?

<u>Nature's Daughter</u> (2005)

A night by the sea,

Time ceases to be.

My thoughts ride the tide in.

The waves carry them out again.

Night after night

My worries take flight

Upon the wind

To whom I freely lend

Geese cackle overhead,

Flying south to a warmer bed

The water reflects the moon in the sky

A beacon of light, to all passing by

As the moonbeams dance upon the water

I am glad, I'm nature's daughter

Selah

"I rest"

<u>In the Wolf's Eyes</u> (2007)

In his eyes

As ageless, as the skies

Truth

Love

Wisdom

Sorrow

Light dancing off a brook

Deer drinking in the shade

Harmony

In hues of red, gold, and green

Freedom

Running in a park

The way of things

Connectivity

Accepting your place

Moving with change

Positions change

Leadership will change

Without conflict

Without envy

Without greed

Without murder

These concepts do not exist

Except to man

The savage unanswerable

Unexplainable killer

Look into the eyes of the wolf

Listen to their tale

Learn, listen, and see

Wisdom,

Strength,

Beauty,

In harmony

With one another

And nature

They do not see

~

Sorrow

A Day Fishing

First, I start with a Palomar knot for hook number one.

Then a drop loop for hook two will do.

Almost complete. A modified cinch knot for the sinker so the line will sink.

Now add some squid and we're ready for fun.

It strikes the water and just like that:

Nibble, nibble, nibble from a small mouth bass.

Strike, tug, reel it in.

Then start over again.

A Child's Wonder

Flitter, flutter

Child-like wonder

Two-tail with wings

Black and yellow

Flitting from flower to flower

Handsome fellow

But not his finest hour

Swish, snatch

What a catch!

Now fluttering, in my net.

And then, in my jar.

I show my little star.

She wants to see

And catch them herself,

Just like mommy.

I let him go,

The show now done.

Her turn for fun!

<u>A Forest Hike</u>

Rustle, rustle

Rustle, rustle

Chirrup, chirrup

"Hey sweet----ee"

"Hey sweet----ee"

A black capped chickadee

And finches galore

Serenade me from the trees.

Buzz, buzz

Buzzing bees

Humming lazily

Walking along the forest floor

What's in store, for me today?

Who can say?

Snap, snap of the shutter

As I click pictures of God's wonder

This is where I feel

The most like me

Now time to pick some blackberries

For home-made pie, tonight

Such delight!

A Serpentine Gaze

Cunningly hypnotic
The serpent lures in its prey
Drawing them in with an enrapturing display
Back and forth it sways
Capturing attention with its serpentine gaze
Swirling, colored diamonds upon his skin;
The wealth of colors lure them in
The snake knows how to win
Dancing, dancing, dancing
Closer than before
The victims never know what's in store
Till the final horror
It's serpentine how the two entwine
Tumbling and rolling
The victim is slowing
Final horror;
The victim gasps for air...no more

<u>Inspired By a Friend's Online Post</u> (2022)

You were the last of your litter

Wet matted fur, in a box on the side of the road

So small and weak, you shivered.

The rain was pouring down

I took off my coat and wrapped you in it

Stroking you gently as could be

Through lidded eyes you looked up at me

And purred for the first,

For the last, time

I cried

<u>Inspired By a Friend's Online Post</u> (2022)

RELIGIOUS THEMED POETRY

Animal Talk (1996)

The friends of the toad

Were gathered to hear a story unfold.

He was to tell of Jesus' past lessons, previously untold.

Within a garden, a long time ago

There were two people named Adam& Eve

Who were told not to go

Anywhere near the forbidden tree,
Whose fruit blossoms were as, fire is to me.

If they ate of the fruit, they'd be told to leave.

Although they were told to stay away

The temptation was there

And it was there to stay.

For a while they kept busy naming animals and trees

For a while they were busy, busy bees.

At first, they tried to obey the Lord

But they missed the mark---

Listening instead to a snake

As it hissed from the dark:

'Be like God. Taste, taste, taste of this fruit.'

They had a taste and to their dismay,

They were caste out of the garden to stay.

As for the snake,

It was no mistake

When God made him crawl

On his belly, no legs at all.

<u>Love (2001)</u>

Love never fails the faithful.

It's often hard to find.

Love's edge can be quite painful

Because in loving you are blind.

Your lover has your very eyes

That see into your heart

So, when he says to you, goodbye

It's often hard to part.

You may think your life is worthless,

True love does not exist.

Now think of Christ on the cross---lifeless!

God's everlasting gift.

True love is a sacrifice

Like Christ's death on the cross.

So, keep in mind this sound advice:

To have love you must pay a price.

Only by dying

Again, and again

Will true love ever win!

<u>Indeed</u> (2004)

If none of it were real,

Then life would make sense----

Why it all seems pointless.

What is real, anyhow?

Something that has always been?

Then that excludes men,

For we were created.

To what end?

To bless the Lord.

      I don't see Him, do you?

Then screw.

      That's empty too.

 What are we?

      Energy: a collection of particles

      That make up anatomy.

Who, me?

Indeed.

<u>Who am I?</u>

I was once "the covering,"

The bright morning star.

Now that I am fallen,

All I want is to mar.

Who am I?

Lucifer

<u>Hindsight</u>

(2004)

As I'm sitting here

The future seems unclear.

Only God has foresight.

That which I hold so dear.

While I have only hindsight

So, all I have are tears.

Life is moving ahead

But I greet it with dread

For what good happens to me?

Only God sees.

He should learn to share

Till then, I guess I'll fare.

<u>The Rambling of My Soul (2005)</u>

Oh, how I long to express

This loneliness…

I regress.

So many wasted years

So many unspent tears

My life is passing by

And I cry, "Why?!"

Why do I feel so hollow inside?

Have I died?

I'm hit. I'm struck.

No such luck.

My life's a black hole

Enveloping my soul

Soon I will be no more.

Just a festering sore

~

As I turn off the light

My world becomes night

And I feel it's alright------

To dream.

I scream-----

He wakes me.

When I sleep,

I sleep

Fitfully.

I'm never free,

you, see?

Dreams allude me.

My day becomes night

And my night?

Turns into fright

As I lose all sight

All sight of who I am

And what I've been.

I'm sin, just sin

Why must I feel that I'm nothing

      Without a man?

And why can't I keep

        a tan?

Oh, how I long I to cry.

I hear Satan's lullaby.

Goodbye. I must go.

I know what you're thinking.

You're thinking, "No!" But I got to go

Once you hear his song

It won't be long

Till...

      All is still

      All is still

      All is still

Have any chills?

You should

For I just spoke a curse,

The worst.

Speak a line

Three times

Especially in rhyme

And soon it will be so

Got to go

Satan's Lullaby

Sleep my darling, close your eyes.

Satan keeps you warm and dry.

Hush now baby, don't you cry.

I'll sing you Satan's lullaby.

Close your eyes

Don't shed a tear

Satan's arms are always near

The world is cold and wet outside

The flames of hell are warm and dry.

Satan's lullaby. Satan's lullaby. Satan's lullaby.

<u>Come With Me (2005)</u>

I

Come with me to the depths of Sheol.

Catch a glimpse of my tormented soul.

Down, down to the depths we go

Where the river of Oblivion, Lethe does flow.

Don't fall in or you'll forget all woe.

Leave an offering for the unburied souls

Then hop in the ferry and pay the toll

Deeper, deeper into the dark we go

Through the dead marshes, don't look below

They will pull you in if you do,

All races of men who've died in sin, calling out for you

So, whatever you do,

Do <u>not</u>, follow the light.

Not even your might

Will save you.

There will only be torment.

Eternal lament

Your time will be spent

Thrashing, gnashing your teeth like a shark

Eternally in the dark

On the tip of your tongue,

What do you taste?

Your own blood and human waste.

Breathe through your nose,

What do you smell?

The depths of hell:

Sulfur and fire,

Burning tires.

All around you,

What do you feel?

  -----The Extremes

Extreme cold, colder than steel.

Enveloping, suspending me in this irky mire

Extreme burning, pulsating, liquid hot fire

And lest I should forget

Ten-foot-long worms, that writhe in this pit

Brushing by me, in and out of me.

All slimy.

To and FRO, they go.

Open your ears,

What do you hear?

Screaming and bleating,

Groans and moans.

All in unearthly tones.

We've gone past the marshes,

And what do you see?

A three headed dog, hungry for me

I throw him some meat. Now he's, my friend.

I've avoided a terrible end

At last, I'm standing face to face

With him who shows no grace.

Yet one thing I have in my favor

"Oh, great deceiver and tempter

Of ladies, great Hades, I beseech you.

Whatever you ask, that will I do."

"Only, give me back my tormented soul.

I've made the journey and paid the toll."

Very well. Granted.

Just as you demanded.

You may have your tormented soul

But it will never be whole,

Lest-------

Heed my one request.

Wear for me this ring.

When you sleep, I'll sing.

Invite me then, inside your head

And lay with me, in bed

When you sleep, you'll dream.

When you scream,

I'll wake you.

No one else may take you.

Then when you die,

Don't cry

But you must exchange truth for a lie.

Exchange heaven for me.

Then you will see

How heavenly, hell, can be.

With me by your side

And you as my bride

Together we will sing,

"Death has lost its sting!"

What do you say?

II

Perhaps, some day.

For now, I'll take my tormented soul.

Maybe another will make it whole.

I'll make that my goal

And if I don't succeed, I'll come back to Sheol.

Thanks for coming with me to the depths

     Of Sheol.

If I can't find another to make it whole,

    Can I afford the final toll?

<u>Things Aren't Always What They Seem (2005)</u>

Last night I awoke from a terrible dream.

I ran to the mirror and unearthed a scream.

It wasn't a dream.

I have no soul.

Since the day of my creation, I'm paying the toll.

There are seven deadly sins.

I just can't remember which one I'm in.

I cry, (but you can't hear my shout)

"For which one of these, was I caste out?"

All I said was, "Lucifer might have a point".

For this I'm tossed out of the joint?

Caste out of heaven to the earth below.

My sin as a shadow, everywhere I go.

No repentance,

No forgiveness,

No mercy,

No salvation for me.

I cry as I look in the mirror,

"I'm shapeless, formless."

You can't see one bloody tear.

I MUST exist, in the realm of night

But I only know for sure when I walk in the light

My shadow, a tell-tale sign

I've crossed the line.

No redemption,

No remission

Of sin.

Knowing where I'm going, this is hell, I'm in.

Lesser mortals hear my cry

But leave without hearing, "Why, God, why"?

They, run from me, screaming.

Hoping they're dreaming.

I hope for that too.

There's nothing I can do----

To return.

"My lesson's been learned."

"Why can't I turn?"

I saw you Lord, face to face.

I questioned your authority.

Me and a minority.

We never expected to be displaced,

By the human race.

We questioned your audacity.

"What about our reality?"

Day and night we were before your throne,

Worshipping You, alone.

Wasn't that enough to please?

"Jesus, your tough," I sneeze.

You made them in Your image, to be co-heirs with You.

We questioned Your motives. "What more must we do?"

We already serve You. We won't serve them, too.

And for this we're caste out,

Still filled with doubt.

"Why not us, too?"

We loved You.

Things aren't always what they seem.

Only humans may be redeemed.

If only I could wake from this terrible dream.

"Selfish, selfish Lord", I scream.

You created us, just to replace us

With human beings.

We could have been good co-heirs too.

We loved You. I *loved* You.

And for this----

You chose to caste me into the abyss.

I cry.

Blood falling from my demon eyes.

Why must I be despised?

Lies, all lies.

Things aren't always what they seem

I just want to wake from this terrible dream.

<u>Darkness Becomes Me (2005)</u>

Once the night

Brought me fright

Now, I greet it like a long-lost friend.

Sending out a greeting on the back of the wind

Once, the dark seemed to envelop me

Sending a chill down my spine

Now I see it as embracing me

Asking me for a bit of its time

Once the cold of the night made me shake

Till I realized it was pleasing like a fresh mountain lake

The fresh chill of the night

Isn't nearly as dire

As the all-consuming fire.

That is, the light.

Cast out of darkness

And into the light

One is said to regain sight.

Perhaps one might

But the darkness

Is more understanding of who I am.

Not placing a label on me, such as "sin"

So here I remain

As night calls my name

Come into me

And I'll set you free

Then you will see

How it was meant to be

The darkness ---------

Becomes me.

Now I am free!

"It" (2005)

"It" was darker than the night

As my mind filled with fright

In Jesus' name I told it to go

Doubting that that could be so

The shadow advanced, real slow

Suddenly…. A spark

"Light casts out dark"

And the switch was by the door

So toward "It" I ran and flip,

"It" was no more.

<u>Beauty is in the Eye of the Beholder</u>

A plus-size woman. That's me.
But is that all you, see?
Are you revolted;
Have you immediately bolted?

For I am NOT defined by society's
Definition of pretty.

They'd have you believe that beauty
Is NOT in the eye of the beholder,
But in the span of her thighs
And in cup size. (42" waist, 42DD).

Hourglass shaped is the ideal to seek,
Which is an unnatural physique
Obtained through:

enhancements above
With some (not too much) junk
In the trunk, below
With spewed out innards, for the tummy, has to go.

Is that truly the best that we can be?

And even if, per chance, you're not
One of them,
Am I just cushion for the pushing
Or some such euphemism?

I am a woman
Created by God
A daughter
A sister
A mother

If your eye causes you to sin, pluck it out.
For image and sexism is NOT what life's about

Give out a shout if that's what you
believe and take back what beauty should mean: daughter of the one true king

What do you see
When you look at me?

God Said, 'Slow Down'

Click, clack
Tip, tap
Whirrrrrrrrrrr......
The world in motion
People hurrying
Scurrying
Like ants, in this concrete jungle
A lawn mower
Cutting rectangular swathes
A patch of green
In between
Brick and mortar
So busy
It makes me dizzy
With sorrow
Too focused on tomorrow
We lose our yesterday
Till we're dead.
Then, on our grave display:
"God said, 'Slow down' ".

<u>Between the Lines</u>

You wink and smile at me.

Did I interpret correctly,

Or see what I wanted to see?

From ear to ear, I grin back

With a smile that reaches my eyes.

The moment ends as you pass by.

I, too shy, to say anything

like: "Are you thinking the same thing?"

"What's your name and do you have a number, too" ? ;

Just look at you

And say, "Have a nice day".

<u>An Unknown Blessing (2000)</u>

A gentleman knocked on the door of her heart

And called her forth by name

He promised her a rose garden

Then he began to tame

He spoke with the hands, more than the lips

And into his snare, she fell.

Enraptured in the action of love, she decided to sell.

Enraptured by the gentleman's beauty

And impressed by his might.

She walked on clouds of wonderful thoughts

And did not question if this is how it should be.

A lesson, yet to be taught.

The grass was green, and the sun was high.

The clouds were dark but that was okay.

Spring yes, but signs of rain; but still a perfect day.

As the watch beeped, the rain fell.

And in his arms, she cuddled.

Side by side against the wall, they sat

Ignoring the growing puddle.

Holding hands,

Exploring, touching.

And Then-----

      Quickly they rushed back to school

         So, his ride would not be missed.

She biked home with a smile upon her lips.

Such fine Roman hands, they could never betray.

Then the grass turned to sand.

Ask not and want not, if only she knew

That the actions of love, without love, is soon over.

God ordained it to be so.

Then with one phrase, she said it all, 'It's over.'

<u>From One Kiss (1998)</u>

Angelica smiled remembering her first kiss.

Tom kissed her so sweetly, she forgot her past.

Only Tom had a love for her that would last.

The relationship between them would grow to the end,

And all because of one kiss.

Angelica and Tom loved one another

And at the beach they showed how they felt for each other.

During the day they had a picnic and played.

Then they went jogging till the sunset was displayed.

The sunset showed crimson on the beach below.

Angelica had a great day but soon would have to leave

As the sun burned out its fiery glow,

He kissed her farewell so at the day's end she wouldn't grieve.

<u>Greatest Fear (Nov 2004)</u>

Performance Anxiety----

Now?!

(*Hold on it will come*)

I see you and my heart sighs...

I don't know what to do.

Your eyes penetrate straight through---

And what do I do?

----Turn my gaze.

To know you,

Be known by you---

Is my one request,

Lo, my

One

Desire.

But

Fear

Is my

Mediator.

And such a chasm

Exists that who could

Cross? Not I, for I am just

A shadow dictated by fear.

<u>Tongue Tied (2004)</u>

Shutter, flutter.

When I speak, I stutter.

If only you could read my mind.

Shutter is the chill

    Running down my spine.

Flutter is the sound

    Of my heart stopping time.

<u>I Will Abide (2004)</u>

To him:

Pitter, patter, flutter, shake.

Pitter, patter, flutter, shake.

My body's all aquake----

Where can my heart be found?

Surely, I will drown in this sea of emotion.

To her:

I will arise and calm the storm

And give your purpose, form.

All quaking will subside

If you abide---

      In Me.

To him:

I will abide

If you will be my guide

O'er this sea of emotion.

To her:

Just ride---

The tide will subside

And I will lead you to the shore.

<u>Fools (2004)</u>

I've failed,

For who knows who I am?

Not he

For fear shut my mouth.

I don't know what *I* want.

Excuse me

But you're the one who

Had to play games.

Who started it in the car,

And put words in my mouth.

What do you expect me to say to that?!

You're wrong in thinking you know me!

I didn't invite you here, "just to have fun", as you say.

You reached out to me

So, I thought you knew me.

We were two branches off the same tree

And you don't want me in your heart?

Then don't start----

The game.

That's not how I play.

I play----

      For keeps.

Nothing's changed.

You're all the same---

           Fools!

Frigid (2004)

Cold cordiality.

Worse than outright hostility.

At least there

The purpose is clear.

A swinging fist

Is hard to miss

But this?

Very shortly I will see

How it's gonna be

Between him and me.

Frigid

<u>Thank God for Doubt </u>(2004)

I

It was a kiss that stopped time.

Only his heart and mine,

Ticking in the silence.

Broken only by breath escaping,

Nervous laughter, and quaking.

One question----

Hesitation.

Foreplay-----

But he doesn't stay.

----Silence-----

I am alone

With him on my brain.

I'm not the same

As this untamed,

Insane,

Idiotic, no brain.

To him it's just a game.

II

As for me,

I'm longing----

For something more

Than to be labeled a whore

For his sake.

That's an offer, I refuse to take.

He stalked out.

Thank God for doubt.

Once again, the ticking.

Tick, tick, tick

Of my heart

In the dark.

It was mine all along.

His tick is gone.

Stopped working a long time ago

Silence is all he'll ever know-----

Till dawn enters his heart,

Casting out the dark

I am on my own.

Alone.

Nostalgia (2003)

Nostalgia Remembered

Of things forgotten

Memories of a

Time gone by:

Sweet reflection.

Sad farewells

Flit through my mind

Like shadows in a sunny vale

    …. Like a hand in a glove

Sadness and love.

Together, they're meant to be.

But when night is done

And the day is come,

The glove is shed

Unremembered

    -----Sadness

<u>A Cold North Wind (2005)</u>

When I gaze into your eyes

I just can't surmise

What you see in me

I'm like the wind, you see.

Always been free.

Anything else terrifies me.

Your eyes enrapture,

No, they capture, my gaze.

Before the haze,

I drift away.

Okay, what am I to do?

If you knew-----

But I don't think I'll tell.

Caste your penny in the well

I'd like to change.

Really, I do.

I want you------

To kiss me, but here's the deal,

What will you feel?

"I fear,

      Nothing."

That's something.

      Nothing, that is.

Which is what I am.

A cold wind, that blows along the shore.

Then dies out and is no more.

How can one harness the wind?

And are you willing to try?

I don't want to make you cry.

Such tender eyes,

Laughing and carefree.

What do you see, in me?

----------Just a "cold" <u>north wind.</u>

Spring Fling (2005)

It was just a spring fling

And the memory still stings

Replaying over, and over, again

As blissful as it was, back then

An all-consuming fire

With which playing, is dire

I was burned

But still, I refuse to learn

My hindsight is 20-20

Bet against that if you feel like losing money

Sweet honey. Eat only so much or you'll have a sore tummy.

       No, it's my heart

       That's broken all apart.

When can we start-----

    Over again?

      >Bittersweet Sin<

     My weakness was men,

      Now it's just him.

Oh Billy, why?

You pretended to try

Then you say, "it's too fast and too soon

    For someone I don't know anyway."

Hey! Why did you play that tune?

You took me to the moon

    And I'm still having trouble coming down,

Wanting you around.

    That's who I am!

    Where've you been?

It wasn't just you

And it wasn't just me.

It was "we", that week.

What more do you seek?

I felt no need to speak.

Action speaking louder than words, I thought.

But I guess I'm being absurd, and you wanted words

So, I'll share them if they'll be heard.

I just don't want to be lonely; now you know me.

Did you want to, or was that a lie to?

My Boy (2005)

Faithfully violent

Never compliant

Hungry at every turn

Will I ever learn-------

To block faster.

Pain is my task master.

"It" defines me,

You see.

He calls me "Tappy"

~

I'm slap happy.

Impervious to pain.

"Pitho" is my fighter's name

Or someday it will be

When it becomes me

"Confident" with the action

To back my fame

Oh, Joy!

Someday…

Hey,

Wasn't expecting that.

Tap, tap, tap

<u>Pain, I Understand (2005)</u>

I sacrifice my heart on the altar of pain.

That is perfectly sane.

     Not-----

I have a catch in my throat, a sob. I choke it down

As I hide my frown.

"Hit me again," I say.

"Let's play."

Pain, I understand

And more than demand.

Blood mixing with sand.

Lies, I despise

Weaving a web of <u>incurable</u> pain

On comes the rain,

Damn eyes!

"Hit me harder," I say.

"I like it that way."

In this web I am caught

Not...

     Like him, I say,

I am honest right away.

Always revealing

Never concealing,

Which is a lie by the way

"Hit me again" (in my head) "Damn men!"

<u>To Dream (2005)</u>

I'm caged within a dream

It would seem.

Trapped within my mind.

I can escape at any time,

But rather not.

Dreams are all I've got.

         .... To cling to.

How 'bout you?

Each dream a token to a world beyond

Where fantasy takes wing upon a song

And there's a prince to embrace you

All night long

Each kiss as passionate as love's first kiss

But just like magic, will never miss

Together you take flight upon a Unisus

         .... Such bliss!

Looking below at fields of blue

Dancing flowers of every hue

Within this kingdom all is known

No waking up saddened and all alone

No secrets are kept from him, by you

Through and through.

You know me too.

And we choose to embrace

In this place.

Contented and carefree,

Just to be.

As I look lovingly into your face...

I wake.

The world comes crashing in

Once again.

But hey

Though I may not be able to stay

In my dreams, I'll be with you

Forever and a day.

See you tonight

(Goodnight)

<u>The Ocean I See (2005)</u>

As you hold me softly, closely

An ocean is all I see

In your eyes, drawing me in

To places I've never been

And cannot fathom

But only imagine

The tide pulls me down and under

How will I breathe, I wonder?

Gasping for breath I cry

Feeling as though I could die

But then you rescue me

By softly, caressing me

And with a kiss, assuring me

The hard part is done.

Now I can see the sun

Rising over me,

Warming me.

All over, even inside.

I ride the tide

Each surge, drawing me

Closer to the shore

Where I collapse

Gratified

~

There is no more

II

That's one possibility

I see, in the sea

Of your blue green eyes

But I'm not sure it's wise

To tell you

For what will I do

If all I fathom

And imagine

Turns out untrue

Musings of a Depressed Woman (2005)

I often wonder who I am

And in thinking about it I cry

Without shedding one tear, I cry….

Who am I?

The rent in his side….

The blood coming down,
Mixed with water.

The crown,

Testify……

I am his daughter.

But this world is dark.

I'm walking down a tunnel

Dreaming of a park

That I never knew.

Why?

Because the serpent lied.

It's true

Now…we will die.

I sigh,

Why not now?

How?

With a knife. Perhaps.

All it would take is just one slash.

But I never could cause myself pain.

I'm too sane.

So, I ponder my death, at the hand of someone else.

But it doesn't come true, so what do I do?

I cry,

Who am I?

    ...As I die

One day at a time, by:

Each lie

The waiting

Hating

Phone not ringing...

(Sigh)

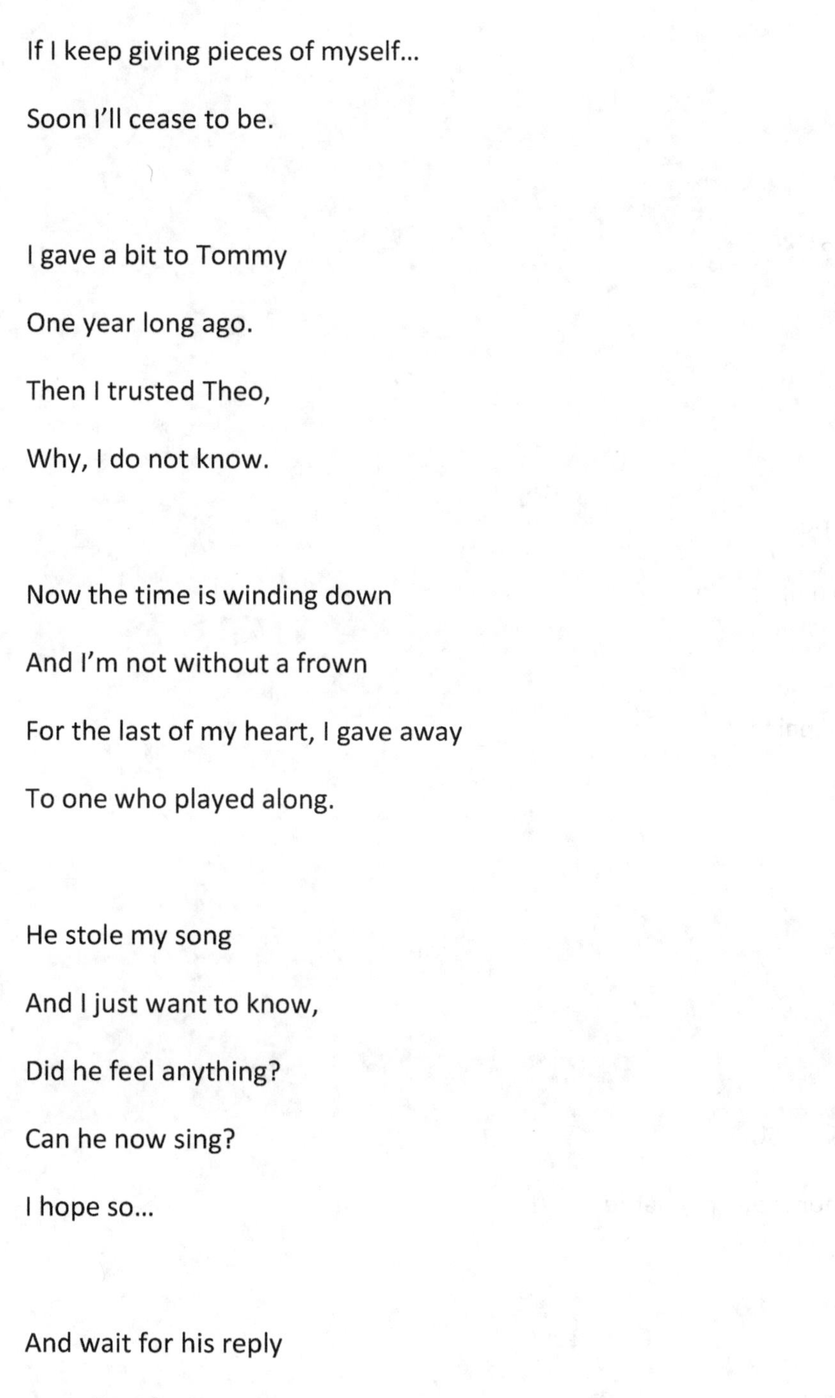

Where am I?

I'm a giving person.

That, no one else can see

If I keep giving pieces of myself...

Soon I'll cease to be.

I gave a bit to Tommy

One year long ago.

Then I trusted Theo,

Why, I do not know.

Now the time is winding down

And I'm not without a frown

For the last of my heart, I gave away

To one who played along.

He stole my song

And I just want to know,

Did he feel anything?

Can he now sing?

I hope so...

And wait for his reply

To...all I asked, is why?

I'm Swell (2005)

You ask me how I am

"How am I?"

Do you *really* want to know?

No.

Don't ask me how, but why?

For isn't that the question of the ages?

Turn back the pages.

I don't mean to sound cliché in this

But I was my mother's first true wish

For she tried, then cried. Tried, then cried.

Two miscarriages later, she was all torn up inside

But then I came

After a night chocked full of emotional pain

For her father had died

And my mother cried

Then came to her, this psalm

Which here now, I read without any qualm

"Weeping may endure for a night,

but joy shall come in the morning" (Ps 30:5b)

And so, I came, and from this verse, mom took my name.

"Joy," which indeed I try to be.

But I have a hard time lying, you see

And I don't want you to cry for me

For, what is emotion?

It ebbs and flows, to and frow it goes

Like the waves of the ocean,

Is emotion.

II.

But you want to discuss how,

Do you now?

"Very well, I'm swell"

The churning part of the wave

Peak to peak

And trough to trough

It's some emotion in the middle I seek

But it's always troughs or peaks.

I'm

Churning, churning, churning inside

Peaks I show, and troughs I hide

So, when I say I'm swell

Well......

<u>Fuck You (2005)</u>

My life is a walk down a dark path

But in the night

The stars are so bright

My soul takes flight

And I track the journey

Of the stars through the sky

Shooting stars collide

And I ride

The star dust brings mist to my eyes.

--------- your eyes, <u>not</u> his eyes

       I see

What the fuck was I thinking?

I just wanted to have a little fun; you see.

It meant nothing to me

I don't like to get too close, you see

Trust is an issue for me.

And you used *this* against me

And what the fuck should it matter

If I'm a Size B, Jimmy?

       Can't handle it? Oh,

I can handle it

Yeah sure, I can handle it

I just can't commit

To the final prick,

Sting, thing

      If it doesn't mean anything

And there you two are

Laughing at me

Cajoling me

Till I snap-----

And rush headlong into your trap

Don't attack angry, they all say

But hey,

I couldn't resist.

I just wanted to slam a fist

Into your fucking face

Because you don't see...

Neither of you, fucking see

What trust means to me

So here I am, pinned

Writhing in inward pain.

And he's say'n

Kiss and make-up

-Fuck- (Before/After)

It didn't <u>mean</u> anything!

That's how I trusted that it would be seen

But no, used against me.

Everything and anything.

     Fuck

     Always…

Turn inward, turn inward, turn inward once more (calm, be calm)

Slam shut, bar the door!

No more trusting

Dry humping

Or whatever….

Calm, I need to calm

But the mistiness clouds my eyes

And I despise, I despise

Those eyes

Mine/Yours

Mine, because they cry

And yours because they dance

As the stars of the sky.

Why?

Why must they taunt me?

    Haunt me?

        Draw me?

Fucking Psi-Vamp

Will you drain me of the core?

Will you destroy my very being?

Till I'm nothing

But an empty, walking

Husk of a being,

Nothing?

<u>Your Teeth (2005)</u>

Your teeth have inspired these lines

I now rhyme

One bite

Sends shudders of delight

Down my spine

You may bite me <u>anytime</u>

Please do

Or <u>lookout,</u> I may bite you

<u>Jealousy or Mis- Understanding? (2005)</u>

Jealousy and envy rock me

Shock me

With replays in my brain

They chain

And lock me

Within a shroud of fog

A graveyard covering

As thick and cold as a bottomless bog

Which I slog through

Blindly

II.

Oh, it's not like that, you say

Yeah, fucking right.

I remember that day

Gesturing with your finger

In that, come hither kind of way

Then you slapped her ass and lead her away

On a nice long walk

I remember that day

And you say

It's not like that.

You don't mean it that way

Well screw that.

    Sure, it's <u>just</u> a roll in the hay.

<u>Remembering Back (2005)</u>

Remembering back to grade school

To be a guy and be cool,

Meant asking as many girls as possible out

All before lunchtime.

That is crunch time.

When they would

Exchange names, numbers, and notes

Then brag and boast

Over whom had the most,

Number wise and beauty wise, to see who

     Had won

        But for me, this game was never much fun

For if a guy asked me out, he was considered unsound

And across campus, the laughs and jeers would resound

So, word got around

And soon there were only those who approached

     On a dare

     Then boldly saying, as if I don't care,

     "Will you go out with me?

     Please say no"

        Oh-----

I must have been

Around eight, back when

Yet, since then

It is still the same

Laughs and Jeers if any say <u>my</u> name

I'm still considered poison, to be asked

    Out

And in my head, as loud as a

    Shout

"Will you go out with me?

    Please say no."

Oh,

Ow!

How, am I to lower this tough

Exterior?

When it's such a

    Sensitive interior

No, it's safer to hide

    Deep inside

    Here I reside.

<u>Ways to Be Turned Down</u> (2005)

"I'm sorry but I don't love you that way,

But hey,

We're still friends, right?"

Goodnight

Or

If I didn't see you as one of the guys

I'd be willing to give it a try

Or

Ah, Joy it's been so much fun hanging with you

I can't wait till you meet my girlfriend. She'll think you're cool too.

Or

Hey Katie, "Isn't Josiah cute?"

"Why yes, and thank you, he's my husband to boot"

Or

Without turning to the next page

I'll have you know; I fell for one who was engaged

Or

What kind of game are you trying to pull?

I thought you wanted to have fun, but I guess you're dull

Or

He'll play along and when pressed, sing this song

I'm sorry but it's too soon for me to be seeing anyone,

For too recently ago, I've divorced someone

And now?

I find that I've fallen for you

And have no idea what to do

For you bite me,

Then slight me

Which irks me

So, I fight thee.

You'll snuggle, then cuddle

But practically the next day you walk through that door,

You don't come back till nearly 4 in the morn.

Then you'll apologize for making me wait

But send me out before it's too late.

Then in excuse for your behavior, you say

"I want you to understand, tomorrow's my long day"

Which of course, makes it all okay.

At least you're not as worse

As my first

Who took everything that I said

With trust, and turned

It against me like corroding rust

Making me feel like

A speck of dust

Which is, by the way, why

I don't trust

<u>Hope Snuffed Out (2005)</u>

All hope is gone

Nothing is left to turn on

Any glow you see

Shining out of me, is burning dim and low

I'm an empty husk of a being

So, any glow you've seen

Doesn't mean anything

It's a candle <u>within</u>

A <u>pumpkin.</u>

That smile you see

Does it look eerie?

It ought to be

For it doesn't reflect me.

I chiseled it out, with a blunt knife

Called strife.

I hate my life

And I'll never be anyone's wife

So, snuff my candle out

I won't scream, and I won't pout

<u>Hope Snuffed Out (2005)</u>

For I've no more treats to give out

Which means my life is forever

About

Avoiding tricks (no pun intended)

So do look out!

For if this is what my life is about

Just you try a trick on me

And I'll break off your stick

Like a branch off a tree.

But punishing pricks

And breaking off sticks

Is not how I want to be seen

I mean,

I only lash out

When what they're about is being mean

I just want him to see

The real me

I'm trying not to hide

And am willing to let him inside

But all he does, is fucking lie.

Giving a little bit, then casting me aside.

It's enough to make me cry,

      I want to die

Yet my eyes are dry.

I'm empty, empty, empty inside.

Though I'm a clown on the outside,

On the inside, I frown

My legs are so heavy, my

Spirit's weighing me down

I just want to be

Happy.

It's crappy,

Being me.

No one should be

This lonely

If only...

I just want to be seen

I want more than a dream

I want love and affection

Please look in my direction

Don't shut me out

And I'll show you what I'm all about

Set me free

And you will see

That I can be

Everything you need

      Indeed, if only...

<u>More Than Blood (2005)</u>

A hollow desperation

Drives me on to satiation

I hunger. I pine,

To make you all mine.

Skin and lips

To kiss

Is perfect bliss

Two bodies entwine

And genes combine

In the twilight

Please hold me tight

And let's dance.

Make romance

As blood drips down

A flower's glory and crown

Crushed

Releasing a fragrance beneath your touch

Intoxication

Lending to satiation

No longer I pine

You are all mine

<u>I Dare Not Tell (2005)</u>

I romanticize

The fantasized

Individual in my brain

Indeed, he has a name

But that, I dare not tell

For well…

I want him to myself

And if I told, he just might leave the shelf

To carouse inside your head

For he's like that you know, good in bed

With everyone else but me

Not that I want him to be

No, it's not like that, you see.

To set me free

All I need is a kiss.

Just to taste his lips, such bliss.

But at least, in my own bed

I can romanticize the vision of him in my head.

No Is Halfway to Yes (2005)

I guess,

No <u>is</u> halfway to a yes

I've proved it true

But don't worry, I'm not mad at you

For wearing my barrier down

This frown

Is not directed at you.

"Then, who"?

It's directed within

As I hit my shin

Over and over, against the tree

It's directed at me

For not being strong

For knowing it all along

Chip, chip, chip away, on that concrete wall

That are my defenses and when they fall...

I surrender all------

Willingly. "Who knows, it just might be fun",

I think. And when all is said and done

It is

Yet it isn't

And I hate it

Self-hate, for giving in

Letting the man win

For not being strong

For knowing it all along

-------I'm weak-------

Which is why I keep men at arm's length

That's the source of my strength

Distance and space

Or else I will lose the race

I'll fall down

And lose my crown

Mean streak

Hides that I'm weak, weak, weak.

It's not you, it's me

Which is why I hit this tree

Over and over and over…

<u>And I Smile (2005)</u>

There is something liberating in letting defenses fall down

I can breathe again

And as I look around

I can truly see again

Such beauty

And I smile

For awhile

Then I sing, for the beauty

All around me

And the beauty beholds me

And smiles back and we

Are one

So, I relax, then laugh

Others join in my laugh

Then they too, are one

And I sing

For it is so liberating

So, titillating

Being free

Just to be

To talk

To walk

And have others respond back

Like I belong

Which comes out like notes

From heaven, in this, my song

Then he smiles

And gazes awhile

Then leaves

And she looks at me, and weaves

New notes into my piece

Such peace

I feel, and it brims inside of me till:

I'm transported with her, "nice voice" comment to the top of a hill

And I'm looking down

At myself, and I frown?

No, I smile.

No Turning Back (2005)

There is no turning around

On this road I'm walking down

The blood flow

Clearly shows

I've had you as I've never been had before

And 12 hours later, I still soar -----

Floating around

I'm having trouble coming down to the ground

Wanting you around

So, I can soar

Once more

I am however, more than a bit annoyed

That I would start my flow

When I still had a week to go

It's not like you stuck it in

So why then,

Would I start so soon?

I blame the full moon.

II.

And now there's no turning back

I'm as horny as heck

Undressing prospects with my eyes

Please me...

Don't you despise

Most unwise

Pun.

But then again, it's all in fun.

<u>The Sky Cries (2005)</u>

I let the sky

Cry----

For me, today

Then I walked a really, really, long way

I may not know what the future has in store

But of this, I am sure

It won't wait

Which leaves me in a dire strait

Because I'm running out of time

And soon I'll be at the end of the line

Which, honestly,

Given the mood I'm in, is fine

I am ready to face my fate

And start over again, with a clean slate

Because to me, he was more than a date

But a constant reminder, he's less than a mate

You see, I can't wait-----forever

So go ahead, and pull that trigger

You'll be doing me a favor

After all, I'm just his back up flavor

For if the other one runs out.

That big lout,

But I'll remain stout

And secure in who I am.

For, I will never fully trust in men

Or fully give my heart

As I will have no part

In pain!

So instead, bring on the rain......

Of fiery bullets

Aimed at my gullet

<u>Your Gaze (2005)</u>

Your eyes

Magnetically draw my gaze to the skies

Without needing to turn my head aside

I'm pulled within a universe, galaxies wide

A nebulous is born

And stars collide

And for a moment I fly

Through your eyes

Looking through mine.

Our souls combine

     And entwine

And it seems for a moment, we exist before time

Then we capsize

And realize

     Time flies------

Slipping away from your gaze

     It's all haze

          And I walk off in a daze

Reflecting on your love-capturing ways

I don't know if I can wait

For fate

To draw us back, one to another

For you are more than a lover,

More than a friend.

When I'm around you, my spirit flies like the wind.

And I don't know how to express

How beautiful, you look right then, so I'll regress

And tell you the unsatisfactory definitive

Thoughts that I had back when

You held my gaze,

     not just magnetically

          But poetically

Lacing your story like twine

          With mine

Creating a picture that will be torn down

Till you're around me, once more

Whenever, in the future, that is in store

I thought, "how handsome, beautiful, cute, your face looked"

But none of those descriptors, seemed to work.

All being definitions, out of some book.

So, I remained mute.

Content to hold your gaze.

 Your beautiful, enrapturing gaze.

<u>Shot Down (2006)</u>

Why do I see death in your eyes?

Why does a bird fall out of the sky?

     --------- It's shot down.

Think about that, to understand my frown.

The bird can no longer fly

     In the sky.

     Nor can I.

Shot down

Shut down

Shot down

Shut it….

     I don't want to hear it!

I knew this day would come

But in sum,

     I hate being right

Long lonely night

In company

     With the shade of the tree

Tombstones as far as the eye can see.

If I look hard enough, will I find me?

No more

       There can be no more.

I knew it

You blew it

       Yet I knew it

       Would be so

You got to go.

"Be"

       Without me----

Be, a father

       Without me----

Be, a husband

       Without me----

Raising a daughter

And loving a wife.

While I,

       Maybe-----

Am raising a son

You'll never know

You'll never love

You'll never raise

An outcast from your life

Like me

As far as a son goes,

We'll see

A daughter, it could be

Or maybe,

Nothing

Like I am,

Nothing

But a distant memory.

I hate being right

Another long, lonely night

Coming up for me

Maybe I'll see

"It" again.

Disappearing, vanishing

Black dog spirit, I see.

Maybe,

It'll come for me.

Hopefully,

     Soon.

Death, come soon.

Can't you see it, in my eyes.

I no longer belong here, anyways

These days.

Now just a dream

Hidden by a veil,

   I always see

     And wish to be,

       Behind.

But I'm blind.

I don't know how to cross it

So, I breathe,

   Shallowly.

     Heart beating

     Shallowly.

Counting down the time

To go, for my life's not mine

I guess it never was

I long to go,

For I don't know

What to do with it anymore

I can't soar,

Anymore.

I've been shot down

There's no will left in me

Anymore.

No love.

He's left me

------Shot down

<u>Inspired by a Guy</u>

Turn back sands of time

So, I can gaze into your eyes

And re-live the past

<u>Follow (2006)</u>

I'll follow you

Where to?

Where?

>Yes, where?

I don't know

Wherever you go

>Wherever I go?

Yes, wherever.

>No.

No?

Why not?

>Because you said wherever.

Yes, and?

>I don't know

>I'm scared

Scared, why?

>Not why, when?

When?

>Yes, when will we go?

>Not where?

I don't know, but you haven't answered my question

>What question?

Why are you scared?

I can't see.

You can't, see?

No, I can't.

And I don't like it

You can't, see? I'm the one with glasses.

Not what I meant

I know honey

But it'll work out

When?

If I knew that I'd be God

I love you

I love you too

You do?

Yes.

I love you more.

<u>The Secret Glen 2007</u>

Desirous to meet in a secret Glen

Beneath the open sky

Dawn's rays in Amber shades

Cast light upon

So many dew drops

Glistening in the glade

Beside the warm, clear water

Steam rising to the sky

Lies a flat, smooth boulder

Blanketed in moss as fragrant

As the sky

And in this quiet oasis,

Waterfall nearby,

Tumbling into a hot spring ,

With steam rising to the sky,

A woman gracefully rests

With breasts as sweet as honey

And golden peaks so fine

Forgetting the pursuit of money

For a nobler use of time.

In relaxation

And contemplation

She wiles the day away.

Desirous to lose the time

And use the time

Wisely, I fly

Down to her

Astounding her, so self-assured

With a simple gaze,

She's dazed.

Grounded to the spot

I've caught

Her with my wolf eyes

That penetrate her heart.

So poised she does not jump start

High tailing it away from me, from I.

Nor does she shy

As I stand, as a man

In all Dawn's glory, naked to the eye

Why?

To take her beauty in

As she attempts to hide her grin

Casting her eyes down with subtlety,

Longingly gazing at my salute to her beauty

She always gets a rise out of me

From the moment I saw her

By the glen

I knew then

And soon she will too

For this love is true

The desire is in her eyes

And mine

But in mine there is command,

For I demand, pussy

Give it to me

Now and always

Adoringly, Lovingly

Sweet human bitch

For none can make my body quiver

And twitch

As you can, my sweet loving maid

Visiting my glade

Beneath the trees

With the ease

Of a unicorn fawn

Not rustling any leaves

In the early light of dawn,

Then moving on, and gone

Your scent lingering on.

Watching you was pleasing

But also teasing

Now I will watch no more,

Together now, let's soar.

Handsome, oh he's handsome

I must avert my eyes

What a beautiful, mystical

Specimen of a guy

The very moon's strength

Is in his eyes

And is that command?

No it's demand

But that's sweet

For I've been desirous to have such a meet

With one so fine

That time itself rewinds

Soon, now, my strength, you're mine

As we entwine, I draw you into my spell

I cast so well.

Did he think, she blind?

She always felt his gaze

Even through morn's haze

But once she saw those brilliant

Animal like eyes, it was then too late

To even contemplate,

Running away as a goal

For they penetrate to her soul

So then together, we,

My love and I, did lie

Upon a bed of moss

Beneath a cerulean sky

And give in

To beautiful, animal passion

I take her

From behind

And we are together, now entwined.

I thrust my member, swiftly in

And then, Again and again.

She moans, and groans

So un-natural is this sound to me.

No bitch has ever made such a noise

As she.

I was afraid I hurt her

At first

But then she arched and burst

And such wonder!

She'd put any bitch to shame

As she came, and came, and came

Then she melted,

Waxing hot,

Not at all what I expected, but more!

Truly with this human maid,

I can truly soar

Higher and higher than ever before

To satisfy her passion, is divine.

How wonderful, I have her as mine

This Glen

This glade

She

Me

Together

Now, forever

Are meant to be

But the secret of my glade

Is for the first time, I was made

Into the man, that now I am

And that's between you and me.

It was she

That made a man of me

And I, a cur of her

Releasing the wolf, buried within;

Her animal passion.

<u>Silence</u> (2007)

Dying embers

Reflect a slate grey sky

The light is dying

And we're not sure why

Loved ones

Few remain

Change comes

Faster now

Unnaturally, I cry

Not one

Or the other

But

Somewhere

In-between

Freedom

And betrayal

One I've near forgotten

The other, I know too well

No mate

No maiden

All that I care for, die

Why?

Out of obligation

And for honor

A human concept, I don't

Yet know

But I will try

The embers

Are my ageless eyes

My innocence

Now a slate grey sky

Neither one nor the other

But somewhere, in-between

My eyes have lost their green

Simplistic harmony

There is now, no glade for me

Just lonely, Silence

"Boy Toy"

I was grinning from ear to ear,
He tells me.
Lit up like a Christmas tree,
As excited and giddy
As can be.
You were his present to me.
My "boy toy" dream come true
Of just 19.
Couldn't wait to screw you,
Undress you, and use you.
Could this truly be?
You were so young and so lean.
He went away;
You were allowed to stay,
Just for this day.

Penance for his past indiscretion,
I'd reckon,
But that's okay by me
Then we
Were one
And when all's said and done,
Over too quickly.

My uncircumcised lover,
There'll never be another.
That was a first for me,
A surprising novelty.

So...
I had you over, once more
And sucked till you blew,
your goo.
Then all energy spent, you stifled a snore
Stating that had never happened to you before. I gave you a first, too.
But I never saw you again
And that's how it ends.

You left and never came back, my young buck that I sucked, with a stag tattoo; I've missed you.

The Blue Lagoon

One evening beneath a pale waxing moon

A mournful cry pierced the night, of a lonely loon.

Its haunting melody cried out to me

And drew me near to where she first appeared.

From her very first gaze, I was under her spell

As into her fathomless depths I fell.

The ocean's waves formed her hair

And her beauty was beyond compare.

I stood there silently, in the night

When she began to sing to my delight.

So, clear a voice, will never be heard.

It echoed through the night, in the quiet of the wood,

Mesmerizing me, As I stood there reverently.

Involuntarily, my legs moved forward, of their own

accord, toward the maid of the blue lagoon,

whose haunting tune harmonized synchronously

with the lonely loon. And as the moon's

luminous beams Lit up her goddess like face, I

was captured in a time before space.

In the darkness, in the deeps

Creation began and took great leaps.

That is what drew me near.

Her story unfolding crystal clear.

All too soon, I joined her in the blue lagoon

And that's where "our story " begins

This being near three moons ago.

She started out slow,

Showing me her world below.

I don't know when and can't fathom the how

When I look back, on that time, now.

As I said, there is no time in that sacred place

Previously unknown to the human race.

Allow me now to lay the scene

As one would describe a dream:

Surreal....

In the depths and expanses of the blue

All the legends are true!

The mighty Megalodon, Kraken, Leviathan

Are sung about to the young

In cautionary tales of how to prevail.

Namely, to run.

Turn tail and swim. Then hide within

The caverns beneath the sand.

And the cities of gold, once found in the world

Of mankind, long ago, have now sunk to this world below,

as the waters and tides rise

Till one day we will become legends too

As earth passes away

My mermaids will tell you.

When one is in a dream, what is seen

By our eyes comes as no surprise

So, I took it all in stride

But what truly blew me away

Is that with me, she decided to stay!

My sanguine Madeleine

Left her tail and said her farewells

Leaving it all behind.

I guess true love really is blind.

Would if I could, it had been the other way around.

But my body was created to last, just above

ground. Bottom line: my internal organs would be

crushed, in a matter of time,

Forever we'll remember the fathoms below

But now are bound for adventure, wherever we go

As I become her guide, to the amazing places I seek

out, where I abide.

My sanguine Madeleine,

You were the first of your kind to leave your world

behind. But that Sullivan trait

To strike out and make your own fate

Will forever remain, in all your descendants

bearing the name.

Every night I've spent with Madeleine, since she's

left her world behind, has been divine.

Now fast forward time...

It's been nearly a year, since first we wed

And still many a tear, she's left unshed.

My Madeleine, so dear to my heart,

I feel we're drifting miles apart.

What can I do to pull you out of this blue?

I say to you, the only way I know how,

"Sweet Goddess, what is on your mind.

do you regret leaving it all behind? "

I murmur softly to you, as we both entwine

Beside the salty brine.

As we entwine beside the salty brine

Your heart beats in time with mine.

You mumble sweet nothings to me

And for a moment, I truly see.

It's all shades of blue

The sky above just a different hue.

Content now to be, just me and you

We can have each other and swim in the ocean too. Go

deep. Penetrate my core.

Soul to soul and heart to heart.

At peace once more, we're no longer miles apart.

Within my cave, you release your salty spray. And my

world's more than okay.

Sonja will be her name, well some day

When the time is right. Our future looks bright.

Joseph, if he's a boy.

I've found new joy. Together we'll create new

life. I'm happy I'm your wife, as you empty

your seed deep inside

<u>Mind in the Gutter (2022)</u>

My mind is in the gutter all the time

Remembering what slickness between my thighs

Felt like...

Moray Eel his way into my slick cave

Then playing peek-a-boo

In the current, in the waves

Oh, wave after wave

Upon the shore

Peaks of ecstasy

And troughs of gasping for air, weakness

As another wave comes crashing down

Tumbled, capsized

Which way is up?

Don't know but I'll survive

Coming back to reality

Here I am inside of me

Just my thoughts and gravity

As work drags on

.........So long

Vivid imagination, I know

But none of that was so...

Gosh, how I miss this

First love, bliss

Time to go home and feed the kids

<u>Galaxy</u> (2022)

Galaxies wide,

    Your embrace.

It takes me out of orbit,

    Into space,

Colliding with the cosmos.

    Dancing on moon beams,

Sliding down the comet's tail.

To splash then, in the reflection of your eyes

    Gazing into mine, with awe and wonder.

Frolicking foxes at midnight

    Your taste mixed with mine, is divine

Two rosy petals, yours, and mine entwined.

    Time out of mind. Silence me, some more, as we taste and

Explore the essence of our core.

    Good night kisses are so much more.

For a Friend (1996)

Tammy.

Good Company.

Too bad no one else sees

What I see.

So much like me

It's scary.

Then again,

Perhaps they do.

Very few are true

To her or me.

The phone rarely rings.

Shall I sing,

The blues?

<u>My Future</u>

<u>(2001)</u>

Here in my room, I'm free to dream.

Dream of my future---

Parent free.

Humboldt is the college for me

Where I hope to get a wildlife degree.

High School's near over.

The year is almost complete.

I'll be going away but wait---

A beat.

Stress comes knocking at the old front door

And worry is keeping me here on the shore.

I need to get a job

So, my parents say

If I desire to go away

My hard work in high school

Has not been rewarded.

Without money for college,

My dreams have been thwarted.

I say to myself "God will provide"

And I know He's always by my side.

But at times, I wish he'd throw me the travel guide.

So here I am in my room.

"I am" and me---

He has a plan for my future and knowing that is being free.

(II.)

<u>(2022)</u>

Here I am,

The future me.

I did earn my degree

But without Veteran's preference points

My dream couldn't be.

My name was buried three pages deep

On a hire list of candidates.

But student debt and bills couldn't wait

So, three years later

Dream having gotten no further,

I got one job after another

Just to make ends meet.

That goal in life---
Never complete.

Now my family depends on me

So, I go to work dutifully

Delivering your letters faithfully

And it seems to me, will be

For eternity!

Se la vi

<u>Lucid Dream (2004)</u>

Day In,

Day Out,

Nothing Changes.

You know what I'm talking about.

     Tests and Schemes.

     War and Dreams.

Dreams Broken

     Dreams Die

     I cry,

"It's all a lucid dream.

What's the theme?"

I walk in a daze.

It's all haze.

I walk on.

<u>A Few Strokes Away (2004)</u>

Too many times has life got me down

And no one is around

To cling to.

I'm dependent on no one.

But someone

Would be nice.

If I could just melt the ice,

O'er my heart.

Yet where to start?

---Their hearts are the same.

No one trusts anymore.

We're all adrift from shore.

Why must that be?

If we would just open our eyes to see,

We could be

On shore, in no time.

For it is but a few strokes away.

<u>Is the Race Lost? (2004)</u>

I see the line drawing near

And as I stumble ahead

The trees pass behind me.

Time slows down

I can hear my ragged breaths

And my heart is in my ears.

It is nearly over, yet----

       Didn't it just begin?

All of life is passing by me

And though I'm moving forward,

I have the sensation of

Going backwards in time.

I'm just running in place

But the landscape is passing by

And ahead, I see the line.

Shall I sprint full speed ahead?

Or is the race already lost?

No one is around.

<u>Howdy Stranger (2004)</u>

The phone hardly rings anymore.

Not like it did *before,*

Out of obligation.

What a proclamation!

But it's true.

I'm no fun to talk to….

Ring! "Howdy stranger", you say.

To you, I reply, "Once you called every night, out of obligation, but it's alright

That you hardly call me anymore.

I don't want to be a chore

You call up, just to see if I'm alive.

Goodbye." Click.

<u>Your Empty Promises (2004)</u>

A friend, I need.

A friend indeed.

Someone who is true

Through and through.

Not fake, like a decorated cake.

Their life, a charade,

Promises falsely made

With so many hollow words.

We'll hang out indeed---

When my body's rooted seed.

A soft downy blanket of grass

On which you can read

Your empty promises.

<u>Summer</u>

Tammy, "Good morning,

Wake up."

     "No, it's 6:30."

"It's Summertime."

     "Yes, it is, that's the point."

<u>Orange County and Me?</u>

Orange County

And me?

------Hardly!

He's not worth my time.

<u>Too Far, You Say?</u>

Just ten minutes away.

Too far, you say:

Give me a break,

Orange County.

.... <u>Words Will Never Hurt Me</u> (2004)

Sometimes I wish

I didn't exist.

Population control is need they say.

So hey, why not

Kill this dullness and rot

To give the majority more air to play.

"You have no friends"

"You're a teacher's pet"

"Go play with your cat"

"Don't sing, your voice sucks"

"Fuck, fuck, fuck"

"Cover your virgin ears"

"Oh no; look tears"

"Cry baby cry"

"Your grandma's dead"

  Enough said.

Think I'll lay down my head

And slide into a shroud of mist.

Oh, how I wish.

Why? (2003)

The sun has set.

The stars are in the sky

And there is just one

Question on my mind-----
"Why, God, why?"

The stars are blinking,

"They don't know"

Each one is saying,

"They are all alone".

Dejected, rejected

And put up in the sky.

Each one winks down,

"Why, God, why?"

<u>Defeated (2003)</u>

Defeated

Repeat it

Defeated (once again)

All hope is gone,

Where is my song?

  ----Crushed down.

I'm stamped down,

Thrown around,

Crushed, but why not torn?

I'm in a bind

And there's the grind,

Nothing can be done

To take it.

I'd hate it,

But take it, I wish

I could.

All hope is gone.

Where is my song?

  ------It never begun.

<u>Sitting In a Dream (2003)</u>

Sitting in a dream

The world passes by

One moment in time

Time out of mind

Drones coming and going

Like robots.

Hurrying, hurrying by----

Lost in reflection,

Where am I?

On a hill in the distance

Or climbing a tree

No cares for tomorrow----

"I'm free!"

One moment in time.

Time out of mind.

<u>What is Home to Me? (2004)</u>

As quoted in <u>Patch Adams</u>, "home is both a place of origin,

and a destination."

Where is my home?

My place of origin, was sold

And my parents' house has no "room" for me,

Literally,

Turned into a study.

Where I live currently

Is in a Victorian house

But that's just where I sleep

As I attend Humboldt State University.

What is home to me?

Individuality?

Maybe, but that gets lonely

Even with feline company

To keep me warm at night.

<u>Silence Before the Storm (2003)</u>

Silence before the storm

Breeds in every heart,

Anticipation.

Nay, fear.

The wind is blowing,

Stop and go.

Through the trees it howls.

It shows

Branches falling to the ground

Shades of gray all around.

The storm is coming.

The end is now.

Must rain, and sleet

And storm allow.

For with the storm

It also brings

New life

Through death

------ In Spring

<u>Randomness (2005)</u>

Chaos,

Fucking things up.

Entropy,

Increasing disorder,

Wrecking things.

Black tunnels

Through dark woods

In my brain.

Fog and shadows

Hiding within

Residing in

The corners of my

Brain. Darkness

Enveloping, disrupting

Any harmony that remains

I am lost

I've lost my name.

Locked Out (2005)

What's that about

No one else but me

Oh, I see

Right through it

All his bullshit

Making up a story about Griff

Not wanting anyone spending the night

Yeah, fucking right!

Fucking coward

A chicken has more guts.

If you wanted me to go

Just say so

You fucking cowardly ho

You're no fucking GI-Joe

Just a Ken Doll

In a fucking stall

Making up shit

<u>Because of You (2005)</u>

Because of you, I am strong

You have inspired my life, my song.

For you've been abused: Sexually, Verbally, Emotionally

By friends and family.

Yet you've not lost your wit,

Sensitivity, spirit

And Charm

Despite all past harm.

In fact, to my dismay

You remain open, everyday

Not closed off, like me.

You're free,

To be hurt, repeatedly

By men who just lust

But you continue to trust

Even when the last one left you and your baby stranded.

You still refused to be branded,

With any name or stigma, one would place on you.

In fact, now you're dating a true gentleman

that loves you, and your baby too. Good for you.

So Blue (2005)

There is sorrow in my eyes

Looking back at me

Is that what others see?

So blue

So blue

They can be as cold as ice

To others who pay the price

Of inciting me to wrath

Who chose that path?

So blue

So blue

What is it that I see?

Unshed tears?

Memory?

So moist do they appear

And something else-----

Is it longing?

So blue

So blue

Yet so hollow

But deep and round

I cannot fathom its depths

"The Road Last Night" (2005)

I'm walking a line

Whether to live or whether to die

No cars in sight

For it's late at night

Yellow fading to black

Yellow/Black

Yellow/Black

Off into the distance

The road goes on and on

Yet leads to nowhere

And when I arrive

I can't remember having left

I follow my shadow down the road

Stretching out into the distance

I wonder what ties it to me

And if it could

Would it choose to leave?

I know I would

Who would want to be tied to me?

No one has and no one ever should,

For what a drag that would be.

Perspective (2005)

Don't ask me how or why

I cry

For someone was torn apart by lead

When a moment ago, he was asleep in bed

Don't ask me how or why

I cry

For a five-year-old

Was just raped by her dad

Don't ask me how or why

I cry

For there are millions dying

Of poverty and disease

In third world countries

Don't ask me how or why

I cry

For little lonely me

Because I couldn't possibly

There are others with greater need.

<u>Trapped (2006)</u>

Trapped in a role

Not ready for

Never asked

Never wished

Never wanted

Not mine

Not my mistake

Not mine

Trapped

      By love

Trapped

      By responsibility

Now mine to shoulder

What about courtship?

      Gone

What about quiet?

      Gone

What about us time?

What about down time?

What about me?

Gone

Losing it

Never chose it

      Did I?

No, I didn't

Stupid, stupid guy

How could he?

How can I?

Still be with him

Wasn't mine

Trapped in a role

Not ready for

Yet.

<u>With My Heart</u>

Writing with my heart

Writing with my soul

Writing, just writing

Aimlessly

Like I wander through

My life aimlessly

Wishing for a change

Stubbornly

Holding onto hope, stupidly

Crying out for the drama

To end, end, end

Endlessly, I cry out

But it continues, endlessly

II

His life's a black hole

That he cannot pull himself, out of

And I won't do it for him. Not me.

My black hole is worry

And I won't let it rule me

I'll be there when it collapses, his black hole.

Till then, I'll love

Just love

That's what I'm made of

<u>Nothing More to Say</u>

There's nothing more to say

It's the same, everyday

I miss you

      Miss you too

How's little one?

      She's a little troublesome

      But a good girl

I'm sure she is

How are you?

      A little blue

More fighting

More drama

      How 'bout you?

I'm blue.

When will it change?

The tune?

I want the peace and calm

Of the moon

Soothing down time

Me time, We time

    Sorry, what did you say?

    I was tending to the baby.

    How was your day?

Never mind

I've nothing more to say.

<u>Mrs. Smithson's Alias, MS Jones</u> (2007)

Emotions waging war

Tumultuous chaos, in store

Irony

Pardon me, I was thinking of someone

Not two

      But one

Not two

      But that hasn't sunk through

      Quite yet,

      I regret.

Wailing

Crying

Alibies

I'll find a reason not to cry

I didn't do it

I was framed

Yes, MS. Jones is my name

Oh, I told you Smithson?

<u>Listen</u>, that's a mistake

I wasn't even a notion at that time

I committed no crime

It's my life at stake

Why, the alias is my name then,

You say?

 Well frankly, it's a different day

And I'm not the same

As I was then

But then again, I've said that before,

Didn't I?

I forget

Let me start again

I didn't sin

It wasn't my conception

It's MS. Jones'

And that's a necessary role

To play, I must say.

There is, still, no Smithson

But I imagine,

We'll see

If there will be

Yet another alias for me.

That is of, Mrs. Jones-Smithson.

If they will listen.

But license or not,

I've got

No degree for you to see.

That certifies me

As a Mrs. Smithson

Till there's a little one for show and tell

At which point, I'll have a note.

Till then

Call me, MS. Jones

For now, that name will float.

Dream Symbology

Why am I dreaming tranquility,

When tumultuous emotions rage in me?

Spirituality,

you see,

Is another common theme,

I dream

Obstacles,

Crossroads

To goals.

Spirituality here, will help me well

Desire for love

A new family

And marital union

Will come in time

So that leaves my subconscious mind

I am urged therein to explore

But how, I implore

Lastly are repressed emotions and

Memory, tumultuous at best, I guess

Of those I see, and need to confront, openly

And not repress the rest

As they surface

But getting them to do just that

Is the test

But till then

I'll dream and see what lies within

<u>Ex-Memories</u>

A broken heart beat

I can't hear it anymore

A laugh unleashing a boyfriend innocence

I'll always miss

Tenderness

Pleasure

A desire to please

And not to hurt or harm

Lending to failure, time and again

Good over bad

I choose to remember

As he would have wanted it

As he would have remembered me

"Keep your chin up", he said.

I can still hear it.

And I promise I will

For you Jimmy, I will.

Not just try

      But do.

<u>Memory</u>

Memory

Both haunts and tantalizes me

Equally

I want you

I fear you

Equally

I love you

I hate you

No, just angry

Sorry

But

Guilty

I should have grieved more

No more

Do I want to

But I do

Don't want to lose you

Yet I have

By losing myself

Already

Friends? Let's be----

I don't want to be hurt again

But then

I would feel so lonely

Without your company

Without you by my side

I'd wilt within

And yet I hide

Far from your touch

Your embrace

As enticing and smooth

As lace

Now, I fear closeness because

I couldn't handle losing you again

But if I don't have you

I can't lose you

Now, can I?

So then-----

That's the state I find myself in

Desiring passion

Touch

Romance

A future

      With you

But I still cry inside

For you've died

And there I would have you remain

In the grave

So, I'll no longer be a slave

To the pain

That you have caused

And could cause

Once again

Men-----

      You're all good at that

         Sadists one and all

A Shadow of a Man

I live in shadows

Who is the man I love?

Is the man you were

The man you are now?

Shadows on the wall

Are shadows of the mind

All is in shadow, somehow

       Now.

Corpses upon corpses

The bodies piled high

Will you kill me to?

Why-----

Do you enjoy killing so much?

Causing so much pain?

I just wanted to share with you

A small little thing

But you don't see.

You never see,

The small things:

The experiences I want to share,

Do you?

No

And your stories

All your stories

Of the things you've done to others

Does it make you proud?

Do you miss it so much,

That you can't give it up,

Even for me?

Is that the biggest part,

Of whom you are at heart?

A

Torturous

Murderous

Make it bloody

Tear it apart, killer?

Kill it

Hang it

Tear it

      Apart

          That part

              Of your heart

Or else

Go back

And marry it

Instead of me

If that's all

You can live, breathe, and see

Constant dismembering

So black

Where is the light?

Which draws you more?

What color is your heart?

Do I even know

Which one is the mask, you wear-------

Villain or hero?

The arguing scares me

As though the serpentine instinct
Dwells inside

With emerald eyes
Just waiting to strike

<u>Wiling the Day Away</u> (2009)

The time is approaching for us to be gone

But there's still so much that needs to be done

Pay roll

Is crucial

For it makes a good point

Here's a guy who knows more than, how to roll a joint

He's a family man to his core

Regardless of what's in store

He takes responsibility in all that he does

Planting and sowing seeds of love

Why isn't payroll done?

This issue weighs on me, a ton.

I'm sure it will happen, as God intends

But till then……

It feels like the day, is wiling away

As I pray,

    For it to slow down.

The Future, Unsure

So much to think of

Just days away

A trial

A hearing

For which, I pray

We've all been praying

Without end

Family, co-workers, church members

And friends

Will she be home;

Home to stay?

This Artemis...

    A daughter

    A sister

    A child, I love

I hope

I pray, she does

For without her

Is worry and fret

An empty nest

A half empty glass

Alanna, so sweet and sure

Bubbles with laughter

As everyone adores, her

She's the calm in the storm,

I hope to catch hold of,

When I hold her in my arms of love.

I know her sister would feel the same

<u>The Blessing</u>

A child

A daughter

A sister

      Restored!

"Mommy!", she says

      And it blesses me

A cough

Drags on

For one day more

Small things

I'm grateful for

The rest......

      Will work itself out

<u>Missing Family</u> (2010)

Christmas is over

It's come, and gone

No more decorations, out on the lawn

Artemis is missing the festivity

Wishing for the nativity

To be up, once more

As well as the tree

But I tell her it's another year's wait

Which truly bums her

Time doesn't soar, usually.

She's also missing her family

For all that they were, and will be

They matter to her

As it should be

But it is hard on Jimmy and me

With her constant reminder

Of: "I'm missing them"

"They should fly"

"Can I fly?"

      "I've never been on a plane"

Will I visit, in June?

Ah man, that's not soon

To her, Sonoma County, is as distant as the moon

And we're getting sick of it

It's like spikes in a pit

Jagged, pointy

Spearing our hearts

Tearing us apart

The pain of jealousy

She never missed him and me

Nearly as much

Each time she went back

To that bunch

From visits with us,

In the past, of: "what used to be"

Now she's sick once again

And talk about bad timing...

On Alanna's birthday,

Her first, no less.

It makes me sad.

But luckily, her party

Has been rescheduled

And she won't remember

Any way

Whether it occurred on her actual day

<u>So Close to Leaving</u>

The trip to NorCal

Is just days away

I can't believe how

Quickly, it came

May third through fifth

A court date

A birthday

Then, she's already four!

How hectic is it,

Going to be?

For her, my hubby, Alanna

And me

A 215 Renewal

Is also in store

And then a referral

We don't want to renew

His prescription there, anymore

What else is there to say

This poem sucks but that's okay

It is just my journal, anyway.

I hope she'll have fun

And still be okay

As we start to drive away

Leaving for her is always hard

Everything is when you're only four

A dying grandpa, she'll also see

Which will be hard on everybody

His name is Bo

And he doesn't have much more

Time till he goes

Pancreatic cancer

Is painful as can be

And it's tearing him up

Not just Bo, but my hubby.

<u>Shadows in the Dark</u>

Shadows dancing on the wall

Are they monsters?

    Not at all!

It's the light kissing objects in your room

Which casts shadows in the dark, and the gloom

Those kisses are beautiful if you could

    Only see

That red glow of eternity

Forever glowing

Forever kissing

Forever free

    Just to be

    A kiss and dance, on the wall

    That you see

Those shadows

Aren't mean

They too, dream

Of romance and love

    Dedicated to my four-year-old little girl

Turned Again

Turned upon, as night is replaced by dawn

I feel betrayed

>   And alone

Her middle name will remain

Artemis and Magna agree

"It's a part of me"

"it's who I am"

>   She said with tears in her eyes.

So, I must oblige

For I cannot disagree

And become insensitive,

Not understanding,

An uncaring,

Mom

A mom, she already thinks me to be

I guess it doesn't matter

If that's not what others

Will see

"Her" mom,

If they know the origins

Of her name.

They won't possibly see

ME

But an imposter, just pretending to

BE

Forever a label, is all

Anyone will ever see.

And what I'll continue to BE!

<u>A Kingdom by the Sea</u>

A fairy princess flickers in the night

Her light is bright

But clouds obscure her flight

And she's buffeted by the winds of change

Winds she cannot face alone

She retreats into her fairy realm

Where she will remain

Till she can relearn her fairy-name

One I know so well

It's engraved on my soul

If she'd only let me in

I'd help her remember again

Then take her to my kingdom by the sea

Where, in time she will see

Is the only place she'll truly be free

<u>My Beautiful Gemstone</u>

Slipping through the cracks

Of inevitability

Sand grinds down rocks

Into nothing

Waves splash and froth

Turning ruggedness to beauty

My little beauty

May only waters surround you

Gurgle

Bubble

Sparkle

Dance

      And

            Play

                Merrily

Let not the sands

Grind you down

Glitter, Sparkle, Shine for Me

And God will help you through

I love you

<u>Trapped</u>

Trapped by the cobwebs of my brain

Coming out of a fog, it feels at times

Invisible, I seem to be

Or how I feel

Here but not here, at the same time

Ignored.

Seen, but NOT seen.

They wish me not to be------

Here.

Just the children are loved

And adored.

Or maybe, it's just me.

I'm not always here these days

Sadness so heavy, it weighs

On my soul.

Losing someone is always hard

But what if when,

It sinks in,

You realize then,

Chances are all gone.

There are no more.

That's soooooo hard,

And I'm not that strong.

Though, I want to be,

I still feel alone.

Helpless.

Not knowing what to do-------

To comfort

To reassure

Not adequate

Sentimentalities never are

He's losing a father

They're losing a grandfather

In a way, I am too.

That, I can't explain

       Impossible

<u>Dark Phoenix</u> (2022)

In the ashes and soot

She resides

Unable to rise

From the dying ember that remains

She's not as strong as her brother

Rising, up on wings of flame

Her hopes and dreams, all crushed

Living is dying, one ember at a time

Till just the one remains, barely glowing

Who can fan the flame of her passion?

Who really understands?

Some can rise, up so high

Into the sky

Achieving their every ambition

While others remain behind, and settle

Lest there is divine intervention

Or a miracle

Some things, forever remain

Unattainable

The glow fades

Dark Phoenix dies

For All the Tears Unshed

(2022)

For departed loved ones

And heroes unsung

For grandparents

Who were there for all our moments:

First date

Graduation

Christmases and Family Gatherings

With delicious family recipes and cookies

We loved you, for you were there

For us, unconditionally

But

I never thought to ask,

Till your deathbed,

What was childhood like fore you?

Wish I knew you more

Not just who you were to me

But who you were before.

You're missed dearly

Even 19 years later

My dear heart

Yo-yo

(2022)

Economy

How fucked are we?

When card declined, for a $2 coffee

<u>IDK</u> (2022)

I don't know, am I shallow?

Because every 'like' and comment

Brings with it, self-validation, and a smile.

Which, as the invisible kid at school, always took awhile

      To be noticed

      To be liked

      To be wanted

And even then

Those friends are all in my past

No friendships last.

And my future uncertain

Is a poem yet to be written

<u>Pretender </u>(2003)

Pretender,

How are you?

Hunted and unloved?

You know no family

Your past is gone

That which you created

Caused others harm

What do you do,

Hunted and alone?

Wracked by guilt

And a bunch of unknowns?

To be created in a center

Boy genius you are.

But no boyhood memories.

No childhood at all.

Take my heart, boy

And I'll take your pain.

Then you'll have the lesser evil,

You'll at least have a name.

<u>Spirit Dog</u> (2006)

I don't know how to describe it

Or if I should even try

But it, clearly vanished

In the blink of an eye

It was not three dimensional

Yet it was personable

That is, it was clearly not real

More of a shadow, or spirit

Disappearing through a veil

I desire to communicate

I desire to follow

But how does one communicate?

How does one follow,

What disappears and is no longer there?

How does one follow if one doesn't know the where?

Sleeping, I was, in the cemetery

Beneath, and in fellowship with, the shade of the tree

Later I dreamt, or daydreamed I could see

The black dog spirit, looking down on, and watching over me

What could it be?

What can it mean?

Is it possible to communicate with it, in my dreams?

This was only two nights ago

Will I see it again, and where did it go?

I want to follow

I want to know

Did it disappear, through a hole in the sky?

And will I be able to follow if I choose to die?

Free Form Writing

Cerulean blue hemispheres

Swirling in haze

Brilliant reds and orange

Flames burning bright

In the darkness of night

Don't get burned

In the sky

Anger

Loss

Tears

Healing

I fly

What am I?

Phoenix

<u>At the Range </u>(2015)

Click, click, click, click

Click, click, click, click

     Snap!

Pull back, release slide forward

Now wait, and breathe

Sight to sight

Both images blur into one

Firm grip, no wobble

Picture window, target in middle

     Squeeze,

     Bang!

Perfect body shot

No extra stimuli

Just me and the target

Sights perfectly on it

     Bang

     Bang

     Bang

In quick succession.

Perfect score.

Re-qualified,

Victory!

<u>Just a Number</u>

Age is

Just numbers

And stages of life.

We all still have strife.

We struggle and fight

To claw our way through,

One day at a time. It's true.

But you....

You have might.

And it's inspiring,

Empowering,

Enlightening;

It's a delight.

And my heart soars

With the eagle's

It roars

With the lion's.

Such passion

I see within

You.

Don't let society

Derail you

For you could be anything.

Your path is just begun.

Your song, not yet sung.

You amaze me

And it's crazy

To say, but I feel I know you already.

So, what do you say?

I'd love to be your pen pal, if that's okay.

Though I'm hardly as eloquent.

You're the master poet, I'll admit.

But you've raised the bar

And I'll aim for the stars

Every time, with each new line.

You'll see, if you give that chance to me.

<u>Treading Water (2018)</u>

There's an ocean

In my brain.

An ocean in my brain.

Tossed by the waves,

I'm going insane!

As another storm

Rolls in, I can't see the horizon

Where can I find rest?

I can't tell east from west.

Treading water,

Where's my Savior?

I must be far from shore

I can't even see the horizon

No more…

II.

Black and white

Wrong and right

That's the world we live in

But what of, shades of grey?

No recidivism

Yet no, "begin agains"

Even twenty years

Down the line, of

"Born Again"

To those who refuse to see,

A person, not a label

Which is who he is to me.

Forgiven

No further sins

Just let him be

In any other country,

He'd already be

"FREE"

Having proven he

Is no longer that man from the past,

You claim him to be!

America
What have We Become?

America, O' America

What have we become?

We've traded away

Our freedom,

So costly won

And gave up our guns

In the name of Patriotism

For promises of security

We gave up our liberty.

And to say that the government's

Legislation is unconstitutional,

Is to go against the grain

And labels one, paranoid/delusional/insane

Terrorism

Now goes by another name: Patriotism

Those who fought and died

With their brothers at their backs

And at their side

Have all died------------

        In vain.

In bondage once more.

The Patriot Act Began

A Totalitarian Regime

And at its head, a "New King",

Not the President

But our government...

No longer the land of the free

We give up our land, our guns, our freedom to:

Our "New King"

And choose,

Therefore, Indentured Slavery

Becoming what they choose us to be.

No longer free!

Time to take back

Our right to bear arms

Granted by the Constitution.

Time to take back our

Freedom of speech

Whether you would agree

With me or no......

There is no such thing as "hate speech"

Filtering and silencing or criminalizing what I say

Goes against the First!

Time to take back our

Lands, unlawfully taken,

In the name of "imminent domain"

People are losing their homes, everyday!

ABOUT THE AUTHOR

Joy Bird was born in San Diego, CA as the oldest child of Pat and Denny. She has one younger sister, Danny Bear (18 months her junior). Growing up, she was very much loved, but living up to her name wasn't always easy. You see, she had been told from an early age that she was the miracle baby, born after lots of prayers and one miscarriage, on the morning after her maternal grandpa's death. Fittingly, her name comes from a Bible verse. Psalms 30:5b "Weeping may endure for a night, but Joy shall come in the morning". In these writings she expresses a little bit of who she is as a person, what she's gone through and what she has overcome. Some are real experiences; others are entirely fantasized but all her writings have helped her through life's many highs and lows.